Contents

WITHDRAWN

LITTLE QUICK FIX:

RESEARCH QUESTION

WITHDRAWN

#LittleQuickFix

WITHDRAWN

LITTLE QUICK FIX:
RESEARCH QUESTION

Zina O'Leary

Los Angeles | London | New Delhi
Singapore | Washington DC | Melbourne

Los Angeles | London | New Delhi
Singapore | Washington DC | Melbourne

SAGE Publications Ltd
1 Oliver's Yard
55 City Road
London EC1Y 1SP

SAGE Publications Inc.
2455 Teller Road
Thousand Oaks, California 91320

SAGE Publications India Pvt Ltd
B 1/I 1 Mohan Cooperative Industrial Area
Mathura Road
New Delhi 110 044

SAGE Publications Asia-Pacific Pte Ltd
3 Church Street
#10-04 Samsung Hub
Singapore 049483

Editor: Mila Steele
Assistant editor: John Nightingale
Production editor: Ian Antcliff
Marketing manager: Ben Griffin-Sherwood
Development editors: Robin Lupton & Chloe Statham
Design: Shaun Mercier
Typeset by: C&M Digitals (P) Ltd, Chennai, India
Printed in the UK

Library of Congress Control Number: Available

British Library Cataloguing in Publication data

A catalogue record for this book is available from the British Library

ISBN 978-1-5264-5688-5 (pbk)

At SAGE we take sustainability seriously. Most of our products are printed in the UK using responsibly sourced papers and boards. When we print overseas we ensure sustainable papers are used as measured by the PREPS grading system. We undertake an annual audit to monitor our sustainability.

2 MIN
summary

Everything in this book!

Section 1 A well-articulated research question is absolutely critical to research. Research questions define an investigation and provide direction. They tell you where you need to go, and even indicate how you should get there.

Section 2 Research questions are designed to provide insights into queries and dilemmas that are yet to be understood or solved. Good topics for research are therefore topics where the unknown is important and the resulting insights are practical and useful. This high utility must be checked against your ability to conduct your research in a credible way.

Section 3 Moving from a topic to the articulation of a researchable question is tricky. Following a series of logical steps that focus your thoughts will put a tangible question within your grasp. Practicalities such as appropriateness of topic, supervisory support, and funding/resources will also guide the development of your question.

Section 4   A hypothesis is a logical conjecture between two or more variables (one dependent variable and one or more independent variables). A hypothesis is not always appropriate, particularly in the case of more exploratory questions.

Section 5   Four steps that will help you to generate your own research question.

Section 6   A good research question should… be right for you, add to a body of knowledge, be well articulated, be 'doable', and have necessary support.

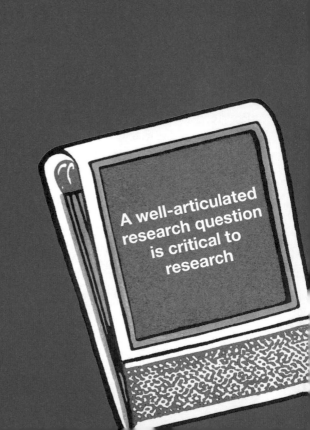

A well-articulated research question is critical to research

Section 1

What is the power of the research question?

summary

**Bow down to the
research question.
It is a powerful beast.**

A well-articulated research
question does much
more work than you might
imagine. In fact, it is
the driver of the entire
research process.

60 SEC summary

Research is a decision-making journey

You may be thinking, 'I have a pretty good idea about what I want to research. Is articulating the exact question that important?' The answer is YES. You cannot jump into your research project without one. A well-articulated research question is fundamental; and your ability to articulate one is essential. How will you know when you have found the answer to your question, if you don't know what your question is?

Research is a decision-making journey. You need to constantly engage in decision-making that is logical, consistent, and coherent. And the benchmark for logical, consistent, and coherent decision making? It's that the choices you make must take you one step closer to being able to answer your research question credibly. So, without clear articulation of your question you are travelling blind.

Research questions are essential because they

DEFINE AN INVESTIGATION

A well-articulated research question can provide both you and your readers with information about your project. It defines:

- the topic (say, for example, youth suicide)

- the nature of the research endeavour (to discover, explore, explain, describe, or compare)

- the questions you are interested in (what, where, who, how, when, why)

- constructs and variables (i.e., age, education, gender, self-esteem)

- and indicates whether you foresee a relationship between variables – impacts, increases, decreases, relationships, correlations, causes, etc.

SET
BOUNDARIES

On your research journey you are likely to find yourself facing many tangents, detours, and diversions. A well-defined question can help you set boundaries. When faced with an interesting tangent, ask yourself, 'What does this have to do with my question?' There are three potential answers here:

1. actually very little – *I will have to leave it and maybe pick it up in my next project*;

2. actually it is quite relevant – *if you think about it, it really does relate to…* (this can be exciting and add new dimensions to your work); and

3. well, nothing really, but I actually think this is at the heart of what I want to know – *perhaps I need to rethink my question*.

PROVIDE DIRECTION

A well-defined, well-articulated research question will act as a blueprint for your project. It will point you towards the theory you need to explore; the literature you need to review; the data you need to gather; and the methods you need to call on. In fact, I would suggest that it is nearly impossible to define a clear methodology for an ill-defined research question. If you do not know what you want to know, you will not know how to find it out.

ACT AS A FRAME OF REFERENCE

Your question not only provides continuity and sets the agenda for your entire study, it also acts as a benchmark for assessing decision making. The criteria for all decisions related to your project will be whether or not choices lead you closer to credible answers to your research question.

Got it?

Q: Why is being able to articulate your research question early on so important?

Got it!

A: Because it is the bedrock of your project. It defines your investigation, gives both direction and boundaries and keeps you on track.

Research questions are designed to provide insights into queries that are yet to be understood

Section 2

What topics are right for research?

A

summary

The best research topics
are of interest to you,
are significant to
the field, can provide
answers that can
be acted upon and
are supported by your
programme.

So those are the goals, but how do you pick an actual topic?

Start with curiosity, with asking *why*. Ideas for research are generated whenever curiosity or passion is aroused. Every day we are surrounded by events, situations, and interactions that make us wonder, stop and think, or bring joy, frustration, relief, or anger bubbling to the surface. This is the rich and fertile ground from which research ideas are born. Think about what stirs you, what you argue about with your friends, family, and peers, and what issues are topical in the world, at home, or in your workplace. You will soon find that research topics abound. If you can learn to catch yourself thinking, '*Gee, I wonder…*', you will have an unending supply of ideas.

Topics can come from

Personal insights and experiences Take the workplace, for example. Just about anyone who has ever had a job knows that workplaces are rife with problems: red tape, inefficiencies, ineptitude, incompetence, corruption, profit before service, morale, motivation, etc. Your own frustrations are often tied to the frustrations of many – tie these to the goals, aims, objectives and vision of the organization, community or institution in which they sit, then there is a good chance those frustrations will have 'research' potential.

PERSONAL INSIGHTS AND EXPERIENCES

An observation Viewing the world through fresh eyes can provide powerful research insights. A student of mine was on a train when he suddenly became fascinated by the unwritten rules of personal space. He was intrigued by the rules that governed who sat where, how close they sat, who moved away from whom, and under what circumstances. He watched people jockey for seats as the number of carriage occupants changed with each stop, and decided that he wanted to study the rules that govern this behaviour.

AN
OBSERVATION

What's news right now? What's the scuttlebutt at work, what's happening in the community, what is the media focused on? The answers to these questions will give you a host of topics. Then you can narrow in further by asking about these topics i.e., '*How is the media covering this?*', '*What is the policy, practice, and rhetoric of government on this?*' and '*What impact is this having on schoolyard racism?*'

WHAT'S NEWS RIGHT NOW?

Stakeholder groups are broad, as are their needs. They can run from the need for an equitable health care system, to a need to motivate students to stay in school. Need identification can come from following media coverage, reading letters to the editor, or listening to stakeholders at various forums including town council meetings, workplace meetings, or any other place where stakeholders may gather to express their concerns.

STAKEHOLDER GROUPS ARE BROAD

It's IMPORTANT to READ!

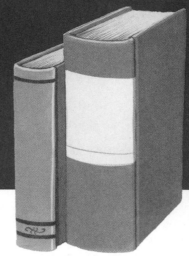

It's important to read! We never know everything about our topic, and rarely do we know enough. Get abreast of the background, context, controversies, debates, and political agendas surrounding your area of interest. You may find yourself drawn to the exploration of an important aspect of a problem that has been ignored in the literature. You may want to question some of the assumptions that underpin common understandings. You may decide to add to a raging debate with an innovative approach. You may want to take up an opportunity to seek evidence for evidence-based decision making. You may want to take up the challenge of answering further questions posed at the end of a research paper.

YOUR TURN...

DO IT YOURSELF

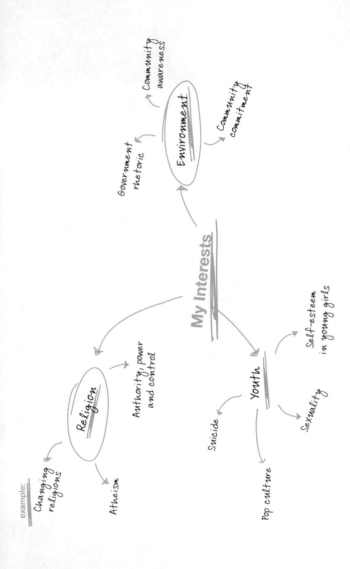

example:

Changing religions

Religion

Authority, power and control

Atheism

My Interests

Government rhetoric

Environment

Community awareness

Community commitment

Youth

Suicide

Pop culture

Sexuality

Self-esteem in young girls

YOUR TURN

Start at the centre, then branch out from there with the topics and subtopics. See how many ideas you can generate.

TOPICS SUITABLE FOR RESEARCH

Here are examples of topics suitable for research.

The accessibility of pornography on the sexual expectation of teens
Selected by a high school counsellor concerned over what he sees as a worrying trend.

A large percentage of non-recyclable materials in household recycle bins Selected by a frustrated council officer in charge of waste management who was undertaking a higher degree.

Violence towards nursing staff in emergency wards Selected by a former nurse undertaking an occupational health and safety postgraduate degree after being forced into a career change by a patient attack.

Bastardization and ritual hazing at university Selected by a student who went through such practices in her first year at university.

Underutilization of experiential learning in the classroom Selected by an education student through the literature she came across in the course of her degree.

Disregard of fire alarms in Hong Kong high-rises Selected by a fire safety officer undertaking a higher degree, who oversaw an investigation where seven people died because they ignored an alarm.

RESEARCH TOPIC

Write down
three potential research topics

1

2

3

CHECKPOINT

For each of these three topics, ask yourself

1
- [ ] Is this topic of interest to me?
- [ ] Is this a topic of significance?
- [ ] Will research into this topic be useful?
- [ ] Does research into this topic meet the requirements of my degree/programme/course?

. . . .

2
- [ ] Is this topic of interest to me?
- [ ] Is this a topic of significance?
- [ ] Will research into this topic be useful?
- [ ] Does research into this topic meet the requirements of my degree/programme/course?

. . . .

3
- [ ] Is this topic of interest to me?
- [ ] Is this a topic of significance?
- [ ] Will research into this topic be useful?
- [ ] Does research into this topic meet the requirements of my degree/programme/course?

Keep crafting your research topic ideas until you can tick all four boxes for each

Section

3

Moving from a topic to the articulation of a researchable question is tricky

How do I articulate my research question?

10
SEC

summary

For a research question to do the work it needs to do, it should be highly specific. Broad, sweeping questions become unsearchable and lead to much confusion and delay. So, writing a good research question is about specificity!

Clarity and specificity. That is what you're after. Clarity means that just about anyone can get the gist of your research just by reading your question. This should be an easy task, but it's often a challenge. Clarity is particularly difficult when you are too broad.

This brings us to specificity. Narrow in. If you are worried about being too limited, keep in mind that *focused* is not a synonym for *superficial*. A well-articulated, clear and concise research question can do a tremendous amount of work. But for it to do that work, it needs to capture the exact nature of your inquiry. The goal here is to avoid ambiguity. Being precise makes the research task easier to accomplish.

FROM INTERESTING TOPICS TO RESEARCHABLE QUESTIONS

Just as a concept map can be used to brainstorm research topics, it can also be used for question development.

In this mind map, the student decided to research the topic of 'poor self-image in young girls'. She then brainstormed some major influences – peers, parents, and the media – and began to think about causes of the 'problem'. This led to some interesting, potentially researchable ideas.

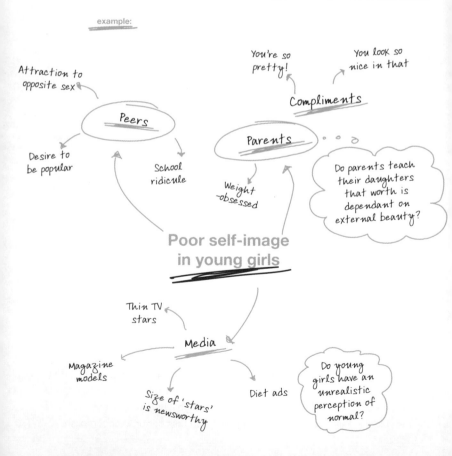

example:

Attraction to opposite sex

Peers

Desire to be popular

School ridicule

You're so pretty!

You look so nice in that

Compliments

Parents

Weight -obsessed

Do parents teach their daughters that worth is dependant on external beauty?

Poor self-image in young girls

Thin TV stars

Media

Magazine models

Size of 'stars' is newsworthy

Diet ads

Do young girls have an unrealistic perception of normal?

After completing the brainstorm in the example above the student went further by asking herself two things

1   What aspects am I most interested in?

2   Do I have any insights that I might be able to add?

From this, the student has two Aha! moments, and research questions begin to come into focus.

The first looks at the role of the media as a whole and asks, '*What do young girls consider normal in terms of body image?*'

The second comes from a reflection on the compliments parents give to daughters, and how often they relate to how 'pretty' they are. The student begins to wonder whether parents are subconsciously teaching their daughters that worth is determined by external beauty.

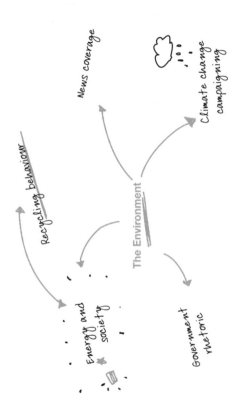

example:

News coverage

Recycling behaviour

Climate change campaigning

The Environment

Energy and society

Government rhetoric

Choose one of your sub-topics from Section 2. Write it in the centre of the page, start brainstorming and see if you can capture things related to your topic like causes, consequences, stakeholders and potential solutions.

START HERE

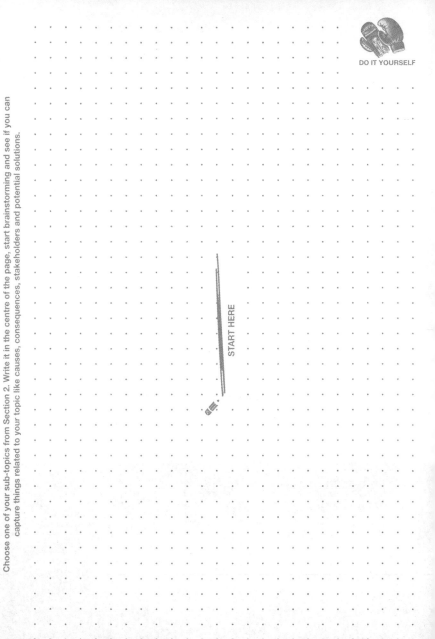

My subtopic is

Found my
AHA
moment!

#LittleQuickFix

Section

Do I need a hypothesis?

summary

... It depends!

A hypothesis is a logical conjecture, basically a hunch or educated guess about the nature of relationships between two or more variables expressed in the form of a testable statement.

For example:

Twenty minutes of daily affection given to a puppy in the first six months of life will decrease aggression in adulthood.

The hunch is that there is a relationship between affection (variable 1) and aggression in adulthood (variable 2). More specifically, the relationship is defined as a cause and effect: specifically that variable 1 will eventually decrease variable 2. And because we have cause and effect (not just correlation) we know that **aggression** *depends* on **affection** – making **aggression** the *dependent variable* and **affection** the *independent variable*.

A hypothesis takes your research question a step further by offering a clear and concise statement of what you think you will find in relation to your variables, and what you are going to test. It is a tentative proposition that is subject to verification through subsequent investigation. And it can be *very* useful in the right context.

Suppose you are interested in research on divorce. Your research question is 'What factors contribute to a couple's decision to divorce?' Your hunch is that it has a lot to do with money – financial problems lead to divorce. Here you have all the factors needed for a hypothesis: logical conjecture (your hunch); variables (divorce and financial problems); and a relationship that can be tested (leads to). It is therefore a perfect question for a hypothesis – perhaps 'Financial problems increase the likelihood of divorce.'

RELATIONSHIPS BETWEEN VARIABLES

Basically, if you have

1   a clearly defined research question

2   variables to explore and

3   a hunch about the relationship between those variables that

4   can be tested, a hypothesis is quite easy to formulate.

Not all research questions, however, lend themselves to hypotheses. Take the question 'How do high school students engage in decision-making processes related to career/further study options?' And *remember*: a hypothesis expresses **relationships between variables**. This question, however, does not aim to look at relationships between variables. The goal of this question is to uncover and describe a process, making a hypothesis appropriate.

Generally, a hypothesis will not be appropriate if:

You do not have a hunch or educated guess about a particular situation i.e., you want to study alcoholism in the South Pacific, but you do not feel you're able to hypothesize, because you don't have an appropriate cultural context for educated guessing.

You do not have a set of defined variables Your research may be explorative in a bid to name contributing factors to a particular situation. In the case of alcoholism in the Pacific Islands, your research aim may be to identify variables involved.

Your question centres on rich description i.e., you may be interested in the question, 'What is the experience of drinking like for Pacific Islanders?' A relationship between variables is not applicable.

Your question centres on the study of a cultural group i.e., you might want to ask, 'What is the cultural response to alcoholism in a South Pacific village?' In this situation, force-fitting a hypothesis can limit the potential for rich description.

Your aim is to engage in, and research, the process of collaborative change This is *action research*, a methodology that is both collaborative and emergent, making predetermined hypotheses impractical.

In short, whether a hypothesis is appropriate for your question depends on the nature of your inquiry. If your question boils down to a *relationship between variables*, then a hypothesis can clarify your study to an extent even beyond a well-defined research question. If your question, however, does not explore such a relationship, then force-fitting a hypothesis simply won't work.

Piece
of cake

Write a hypothesis for the following questions.
If a hypothesis is not appropriate, state why…

1   Is there a relationship between the hours teenagers spend on
    social media and their self-esteem?

2   How do returned service people with post traumatic stress disorder
    (PTSD) deal with questions about their condition?

3   What career pathways are available for students
    who do not wish to attend university?

4   Do pre-school children who eat fish a minimum of three times a week
    perform better in dexterity tests than non-fish eaters?

4 Eating fish at least three times a week will cause preschool children to have greater dexterity than peers who do not consume fish regularly... **OR** Eating fish at least three times a week will not cause preschool children to have greater dexterity than peers who do not regularly consume fish.

3 This is an exploratory question that aims to identify variables, rather than test them, so not suitable for a hypothesis.

ANSWERS

1 Teens who spend more than 20 hours a week on social media have lower levels of self-esteem than peers spending less than... **OR** Teens who spend more than 20 hours a week on social media have higher levels of self-esteem... **OR** There is no relationship between spending more than 20 hours a week on social media to levels of self-esteem in teens.

2 'How' questions are about processes and rarely suitable for a hypothesis.

SECTION

5

DIY: WRITE YOUR RESEARCH QUESTION

Follow this **FOUR STEP** process for generating your research question.

#LittleQuickFix

Using only one- or two-word answers lay out all your important variables, including topic, context, objective, question type, potential relationships. Start by answering the following questions.

Step

1

*start from your **aha** moment*

What is your topic? i.e., back pain, recycling, independent learning, social media bullying...

What is the context for your research? i.e., a school, local authority, hospital, community...

C   **What do you want to achieve?** i.e., to discover, to describe, to change, to explore, to explain...

D   **What is the nature of your question?** i.e., a what, who, where, how, when, or why question?

E   **Are there potential relationships you want to explore?** i.e., impacts, increases, decreases, relationships, correlations, causes...

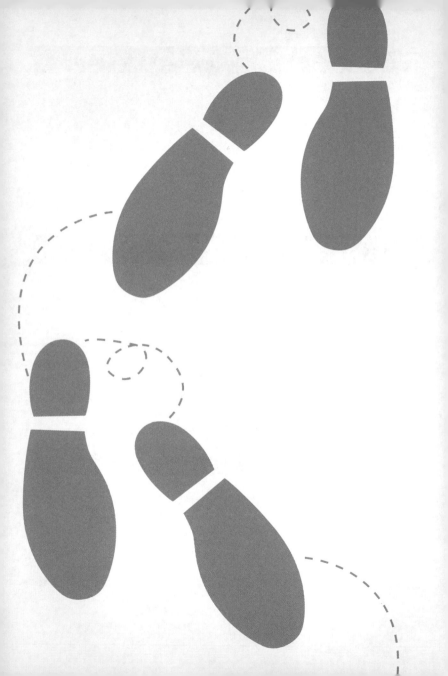

Starting with the nature of the question – *who, what, why, where, how, when* – begin to piece together the answers generated in Step 1 until you feel comfortable with the eventual question or questions.

2

Suppose the problem you are interested in is increased viewing of pornography among high school students. The answers from Step 1 might lead to several questions:

example:

Topic: pornography
Context: high school
Goal: to explore prevalence of watching porn
Nature of your question: how much/ often
Relationship: N/A

Question: How prevalent is watching pornography among high school students?

Topic: pornography
Context: high school
Goal: to understand how porn changes sexual expectations
Nature of your question: how
Relationship: watching porn and expectations

Question: How does watching pornography change sexual expectations among high school students?

Topic: pornography
Context: high school
Goal: to understand education programmes in high school that address porn viewing
Nature of your question: what
Relationship: N/A.

Question: What education programmes have been shown to have a positive impact on the pornography viewing habits of high school students?

YOUR TURN...

Write down the answers from step 1 for your research topic

Potential question 1:

....

Topic: ....

Context: ....

Goal: ....

Nature of your question: ....

Relationship: ....

....

Topic: ....

Context: ....

Goal: ....

Nature of your question: ....

Relationship: ....

Potential question 3:

....

Topic: ....

Context: ....

Goal: ....

Nature of your question: ....

Relationship: ....

sweet

Decide on your main question, based on interest and practicalities, as well as the advice of your supervisor. On the next page, write it down.

3

MY DRAFT QUESTION IS...

Write it down!

#LittleQuickFix

Circle each term in your question to make sure it is clear and unambiguous. Jot down any potential ambiguities in each term that you've circled. Narrow and clarify until your question is as concise and well-articulated as possible. Remember: the first articulation of any research question is unlikely to be as clear, helpful, and unambiguous as the third, fourth, or even fifth attempt.

4

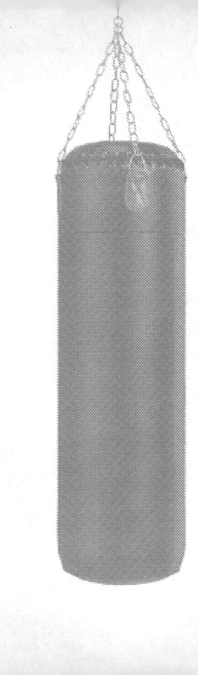

YOUR TURN...

to get to a working question!

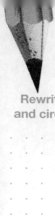

Rewrite your draft question from Step 3
and circle terms that could be ambiguous

Clarify your terms

1

2

3

4

Now redraft your question

CONGRATULATIONS! YOU NOW HAVE A WORKING RESEARCH QUESTION

#LittleQuickFix

A good research
question should
be well articulated

How do I know if my question is any good?

The best way to determine
the soundness of your
research question
is to assess it against
criteria designed to
determine significance
and 'researchability'.

To know if your research question has the right focus and will work for you, mentally go through a checklist for 'good' questions.

Is the question right for me? Being genuinely interested in your topic can help you stay on track, but you will also need to manage any potential biases. *Is the question right for the field?* This will help you determine the significance of your research and what contribution it will make to a wider audience. *Is the question well articulated?* A good question is clearly defined and has no ambiguous terms. *Is the question doable?* You need to be able to access answers. Not only can you be thwarted by a lack of resources, some questions simply can't be answered through research processes. *Does the question get the tick of approval from those in the know?* Get advice. Check with your supervisor before submitting your research question for approval.

Is the question right for me?

Can your research question hold your interest for the duration? You're likely to need a genuine interest to stay on track. *However*, questions that can sustain your interest often bring out your biases and subjectivities. These will need to be managed so that the integrity of the research process can be ensured. Two types of question to avoid:

1   Questions on topics where you have an axe to grind. Deep-seated prejudices do not generally lend themselves to credible research.

2   Questions on topics that are too close to home, such as domestic violence or sexual abuse. While researching such issues can be healing, mixing personal and professional motivations can potentially be detrimental to both agendas.

Is the question right for the field?

The role of research is *knowledge advancement* in a field; *situation improvement*; or *problem resolution*. Research questions need to be significant: not only to you, but to a wider audience. When it comes to your research question, you should be able to articulate:

- why the knowledge is important

- what the significance is

- how the findings will be utilized

- what improvements may derive from the research.

Is the question well-articulated?

Not only does the research question tell you what you want to know, it also points to the data you need to gather, and the methods you need to adopt. This means terms need to be unambiguous and clearly defined. Your question should also be free of unwarranted assumptions. Asking what someone likes about modern art, for example, assumes they know what it is. Remember that the more clarity in the question, the more work the question can do, making the direction of the study that much more defined.

Is the question doable?

The main criterion of any good research question is that you can undertake the research necessary to answer that question. That may sound obvious, but some questions *cannot* be answered through research. Take the question 'Does a difficult labour impact on a newborn's ability to love its mother?' Not researchable. For one, how do you define 'love'? And even if you could define it, how would you measure a newborn's ability to love? And even if you could do that, how would you correlate that ability to love to a difficult labour? Interesting question, but not researchable.

Other questions might be researchable in theory, but not in practice. Research projects are often constrained by a lack of time, funds, expertise, access, and ethical clearance.

Does the question get the tick of approval from those in the know?

When it comes to articulating the final question, it makes sense to ask the advice of those who know and do research. Most supervisors have a wealth of research and supervisory experience, and generally know what questions are 'researchable'. Run your question past lecturers in the field, your supervisor, and any experts you may know.

Time to assess your question

Is the question right for you?

Will the question hold my interest?   **Yes / No**

Can I manage any potential
biases/subjectivities I may have?   **Yes / No**

Is the question right
for the field?

Will the findings be considered significant?   **Yes / No**

Is the cost likely to be within my budget?   **Yes / No**

Can potential ethical problems be
avoided/ circumvented?   **Yes / No**

Is the question well-articulated?

Are the terms well defined?   **Yes / No**

Are there any unchecked assumptions?   **Yes / No**

CHECKPOINT

Is the question doable?

Can information be collected in an attempt
to answer the question?   **Yes / No**

Do I have the skills and expertise
necessary to access this information?   **Yes / No**
If not, can the skills be developed?   **Yes / No**

Will I be able to get it all done within my time constraints? **Yes / No**

Are costs likely to exceed my budget?   **Yes / No**

Are there any potential ethical problems?   **Yes / No**

Does the question get the tick of approval from those in the know?

Does my supervisor think I am on the right track?   **Yes / No**

Do experts in the field think my question is
relevant/important/doable?   **Yes / No**

...YOU'VE DONE IT!

MY RESEARCH QUESTION IS:

To help ensure you have mastered all you need to know to write a good research question, work through this checklist

☐ Do you understand the significance of the research question and the work that it can accomplish in your research endeavour? If not, go back to page 7.

☐ Have you been able to brainstorm a topic for your research that is both interesting to you and appropriate to your degree? If not, go back to page 19.

HOW TO KNOW
YOU
ARE
DONE

☐ Have you been able to articulate a working research question that you are comfortable with and meets course requirements? If not, go back to page 37.

☐ Have you assessed whether your research project would be enhanced by developing a hypothesis, and if so, have you attempted to construct one? If not, go back to page 49.

☐ Have you run your draft question through the assessment criteria and been able to refine your question appropriately? If not, go back to page 85.

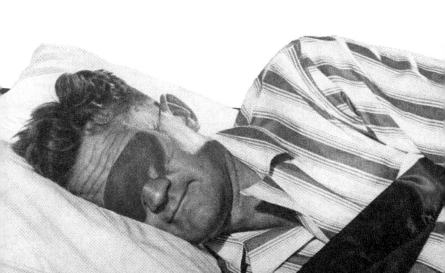

Glossary

Action research Research strategies that tackle problems in participatory and collaborative ways. Action research produces change and knowledge in an integrated fashion through a cyclical process.

Evidence-based Describes decisions and strategies that are supported by scientific research.

Hypothesis Logical conjecture about the nature of relationships between two or more variables expressed in the form of a testable statement.

Methodology Macro-level frameworks that offer principles of reasoning associated with particular paradigmatic assumptions. Examples here include scientific method, ethnography and action research.

Methods The actual micro-level techniques used to collect and analyse data.

Research The systematic study of materials and sources to establish facts and reach new conclusions.

Research tools Devices used in the collection of research data, such as questionnaires, observation checklists and interview schedules.

Research topic The subject or issue that a researcher is interested in when conducting research. Generally broader than the eventuating research question.

Research question What you wish to find out through your research process.

Stakeholders Individuals and groups that affect and/or are affected by an organization and its activities.

Variables Constructs that have more than one value; variables can be *hard* (e.g., gender, height or income) or *soft* (e.g., self-esteem, worth, political opinion).

Dependent variables Things you are trying to study, or what you are trying to assess; for example, in the hypothesis 'Income is dependent on level of education', *income* would be the dependent variable.

Independent variables The things that might be causing an effect on the things you are trying to understand; for example, in the hypothesis 'Income is dependent on level of education', *education* would be the independent variable.